SO-AQD-423

by Julie Verne
illustrated by Anne Kennedy

Copyright © by Harcourt, Inc.

All rights reserved. No part of this publication may be reproduced or transmitted in any form or by any means, electronic or mechanical, including photocopy, recording, or any information storage and retrieval system, without permission in writing from the publisher.

Requests for permission to make copies of any part of the work should be mailed to the following address: School Permissions, Harcourt, Inc., 6277 Sea Harbor Drive, Orlando, Florida 32887-6777.

HARCOURT and Harcourt Logo are registered trademarks of Harcourt, Inc.

Printed in the United States of America

ISBN 0-15-317203-7 – Our Town

Ordering Options
ISBN 0-15-318590-2 (Package of 5)
ISBN 0-15-316985-0 (Grade 1 Package)

2 3 4 5 6 7 8 9 10 179 02 01 00

Hello, I'm Sam. I live in a part of the world called the United States of America. That is the name of my country.

1

Come see my town. It is a
special place. You can meet
some of my friends.

2

"Hello, Jim. Hello, Kate."
Jim and Kate are my
friends. They have a special
job here in town. They help
people.

"Hello, Jake."

Jake is my friend. He has a special job here in town. He keeps our town safe.

"Hello, Pam."

Pam is my friend. She has
a special job here in town.
She brings letters to people.

5

"Hello, Pepe."

Pepe is my friend. Pepe
has a special job that I like!
He bakes cakes and cookies.

6

"Hello, Bess."

Bess is my friend. She has
a special job here in town.
She picks up cans and glass.

"Hello, Gabe."

Gabe is my friend. She has a special job here in town. She fixes the roads.

"Hello, Dr. Fong."

Dr. Fong is my friend. He
has a special job here in
town. He helps sick animals.

"Hello, Mrs. Smith."

Mrs. Smith is my friend.
She has a special job here in
town. She is a teacher.

10

I showed you my town.
You met some of my friends.
You found out about their
special jobs.

Now tell me about your town. Where on this Earth do you live? Who are your friends? What special jobs do they have?

Teacher/Family Member ....

On a Map

Have your child draw a make-believe map of Sam's town, showing the places where his friends work.

 School-Home Connection

Invite your child to read *Our Town* to you. Then talk about people your child sees in your town and the jobs they have.

Word Count:	237
Vocabulary Words:	Earth
	world
	United States of America
	country
	town
	place
	special
Phonic Elements:	Long Vowel: /ā/a-e
	name
	Kate
	Jake
	bakes
	cakes
	Gabe

....

TAKE-HOME BOOK
Welcome Home
Use with "Me on the Map."